My Cinderella Story

"Living in your reality instead of the dream."

By Dr. Cynthia J. Moss

Published by G Publishing LLC

ISBN: 979-8-9894404-8-1

Published and Printed in the United States of America

Table of contents

Foreword

Many years ago, in 529 A.D. Saint Benedict established the Monastery of Monte Cassino. From its start, it has been devastated at least four times, with the last destruction occurring during World War II. Interestingly enough, there is a Latin phrase listed on the Monastery's coat of arms, "Succisa Virescit." The literal translation means "having been cut down, it flourishes." It also means "What is Cut Down, Grows Back Stronger." In both cases, the meanings are readily applied to the management of grapevines in a vineyard. It's a common practice for grapevines to be brutally and drastically cut back each year to produce a bountiful harvest of grapes to produce wine. In fact, no radical pruning, no harvest.

I am compelled to apply this Latin phrase, "Succisa Virescit," to my lovely wife, Cynthia J. Moss. Why? Because after life's tragic experiences diminished and debased her, the grace of God brought her a miraculous resurrection and launched her to new levels of fruitfulness. In fact, she is the epitome of beauty and charm both inside and out. Her speech and deportment reflect the giving and loving nature of God. Absence her sharing her story, there are no clues about the years of abuse and unfaithfulness that she had to endure. Yes, I do feel very privileged and honored by our Lord to walk hand in hand with this chosen vessel of God in the bonds of marriage and ministry.

It is amazing how God can take a person's misery and convert it into a ministry that can set others free. I urge each reader to embrace Cynthia's message of hope, redemption, and encouragement. If you are faced with impossible odds, perplexing situations, or seemingly insurmountable mountains, please grab hold of this faith-producing message contained within this book. Others have been so richly blessed by her inspiring message.

Now, let me bring you closer into our hearts and share a bit of our back story. Cynthia and I have been married for a little over two years at the time of this writing. My first wife died years ago from a complication of Multiple Sclerosis; therefore, I was alone after 34 years of marriage. This time alone allowed me to devote myself to prayer and to fast about my future. It was during this season of prayer that God revealed to me that Cynthia was to be my next wife. Little did I realize that during this same time, her time of aloneness, God was opening her heart to love again. To make a long story short, God gave us both a brand-new start in life, a resurrection. To each of you, "Succisa Virescit" as you read this book offered by a person who has the heart and favor of God.

The Beginning of Something New

It was a cool Christmas day, and as I gazed in the mirror, I was grateful for the woman I had become and was anxious for the proceedings of the day. You see, it was my wedding day, and I could hardly believe that I had been so blessed with such a wonderful man, and after all, I had gone through to get to this point, I knew that I was truly blessed. I needed everything to be perfect on this day, but the one person I missed the most, my mother, would not be in attendance physically, but in the spirit, she was with me. I heard her still small voice whisper, "You are so beautiful." As a tear rolled down my cheek, I smiled. The memories of her flooded my mind. I am grateful to have been blessed with a wonderful mother, taken away from me much too soon.

I looked around, and I was alone, standing there in my beautiful dress and veil, holding my flowers, and thinking how perfect my makeup looked on my face. I still couldn't believe that this day was here, all the preparation, and I thought, "Am I ready?" Everything I had prayed for all those years was finally coming to pass.

The pain was behind me, and life as I knew it was beautiful, and I knew this was only the beginning. The darkness of the past had blown over, and it was time for the healing to begin. You see, this is my Cinderella story, the one where Prince Charming comes and takes me away. I had prayed to the Lord that if He gave me a man who loved Him, then he would surely know how to love me, and the Lord was so kind as to give me just what I wanted. But why wouldn't He? God loves me so much and only wants the best for me.

As the time drew near for me to walk down the aisle, I took another look in the mirror. What I didn't see was that woman who had been beaten down all those years by the circumstances of her past. What I saw was a strong, beautiful woman, one who had overcome some very big obstacles in her life. A woman full of life determined to be happy and accept the blessings that God had given to her. A woman who knew that with God, all things were possible, and she was finally ready to accept the good in her life and walk forward into the future of her dreams. You see, your dream can be your reality if you are willing to walk through your process. This means never giving up and trusting God that His plans and His ways are always right, especially when you don't see and can't understand what He is doing in your life.

As I reflect on the past and all the obstacles that I faced, I realize now that everything really did work out for my good. ***Romans 8:28 says, "And we know that all things work together for good to them that love God, to them who are called according to his purpose" (KJV).*** It is hard to understand this concept when you are going through a hard and hurtful situation. We don't want to hear that all will be well in the end; platitudes fall on deaf ears, and we just want the situation to be fixed and the pain to go away. Through the pain that I endured, the physical and mental abuse, the affairs, and the child born out of an affair, I know now what God has called me to do. He has called me to minister to other women, to help them through the pain, to be a living witness that things will be ok, and to give reassurance that they too can get through any hurtful situations that plague their lives. How do you survive the reality of the present while keeping the dream of your envisioned life alive? Trust God and do not lean to your own understanding. God knows best, and you have to believe that there can also be a happy ending to your story, just as it was in mine.

You Stole My Heart

You stole my heart when my attention was elsewhere. While focused on the pain, I turned around, and you were there. It was at that first glance when our eyes met that my heart started to melt.

You stole my heart right before my eyes, and I couldn't have imagined that you would be my prize. When I wasn't looking, you came into my life, and you stole my heart away.

You stole my heart when I wasn't looking or paying attention. It's like a dream, or is it a reality, the object that I have been missing?

Unexpected that's what you were, my life has been changed, and my past is a blur. You stole my heart, and my heart is yours; never will another come through this door.

All because when I wasn't looking, you came in and stole my heart away.

The Dream

Dream: A series of thoughts, images, and sensations occurring in a person's mind while awake or during sleep.

As little girls, we dream of having it all; the handsome husband, beautiful children, a pretty house complete with the white picket fence, and the job of our dreams. But how many of us truly know life doesn't always turn out that way? We encounter roadblocks along the way that we never expected, and when you don't seek God about the person you should marry, the job you should take, or wisdom for raising your children, things can turn out gravely different from your expectations. As I reflect on the time of my first marriage, I now know we were too young to jump into this thing called marriage. When you are young, and in love, naysayers with warnings are ignored. You feel like you know it all when the reality of it is; that you know nothing. Your only marriage models are your parents and those in your immediate circle to get an idea of how things should or shouldn't be. I had a 1 ½-year-old daughter going into the marriage, and after the end of the first year, my son was born, so I had my hands full. We had left the state of Michigan as a military family, and it was also at the end of this first year that the abuse started. It was mild at first, an argument with things being thrown. As things progressed, the situation worsened. We were young and not in church, but I knew better. I was raised in the church but had allowed myself to stray due to my family duties and being in an unfamiliar place, which did not help my situation at all. I thought things would get better, "I can deal with this," I said, "If I just keep the peace, things will get better." Not only did things not get better, but they also got progressively worse. After each incident, the same promise was made: "It won't happen again." I believed it because I wanted it so badly to work. By the time my son was eight months old, I was pregnant again and gave birth to another beautiful daughter. So here I am, a young mother of three, in a marriage that was not at all how I had dreamed, but you do what you must, so you can survive, and I was determined not to have a failed marriage if I could help it. I was so determined that I stayed married for twenty-three years, in a very unhealthy relationship, always hoping things would get better, but that never happened. With each passing year, it got progressively worse.

Matthew 7:7 says, "Ask, and it shall be given you; seek, and ye shall find; knock, and it shall be opened unto you" (KJV). God is only a prayer away, waiting for you to talk to Him, so he can give you the guidance you need to get through all the situations you will face. While I knew this, I did not seek God on the tenets of my first marriage. Had I sought God instead of doing things my way, could my life have been different? At first, I beat myself up about it, and said things like, "Look at how my life had turned out." I didn't understand why I was experiencing the pain and heartache that went along with my reality. What I didn't see was that my pain had a purpose. I needed to go through the hardships because it made me who I am. It strengthened me, so I can be strong for someone else and let them know they are not alone. Never will I allow another woman to go through what I did alone. On several occasions, the Lord has brought women to me with whom I have had to share my story in its entirety or sometimes only a part. These women were hiding the pain just as I did and daily were coping with their reality just trying to survive. I hope that telling my story will bring encouragement and strength to someone who really needs it. Ultimately knowing that you don't have to be stuck, you are not alone, and that you can believe that God will bring you through. It may or may not be the way you want it to be, but it will be God's best for you and the will that He has for your life.

For example, I was praying for my past marriage to be healed and restored, ultimately resulting in a happy and healthy relationship. God already knew that what I was asking for in that relationship was not going to happen. I often asked myself why I stayed so long but what I realized is that it was my test, the reason behind my growth. It was the one thing that caused me to run to God and learn how to trust and be dependent on Him. The process taught me how to recognize and appreciate the next relationship I would be in. The process also brought me peace, unlike anything I had ever experienced before. Had I not gone through what I did, I would not have grown or even had this testimony for someone who needs to hear it. My pain had a purpose, and it taught me that it is never too late to start over. Therefore, your will needs to align with what God's will is for your life.

I love the story about the potter and the clay coming from Jeremiah chapter 18, starting with verse 3. It says, "So I went down to the potter's house, and I saw him working at the wheel. But the pot he was shaping from the clay was marred in his hands; so, the potter formed it into another pot, shaping it as seemed best to him. We are clay in the potter's hand, and everything we experience shapes us on the potter's wheel. We start as a lump of clay, but by the end, we are transformed into a beautiful vessel, restored and made new. The new vessel looks vastly different from its beginning state on the potter's wheel. The process shifts us, shapes us, and causes us to evolve and be transformed. In Jeremiah 18:6, the Lord says, "Like clay in the hand of the potter, so are you in my hand." God wants to shape us into the people He has called us to be, but we must be willing, open, and obedient to His molding.

What did I learn from going through my process? First, you shouldn't despise your process, and you cannot enjoy the end results without going through the process. There is no downtime with God, and He is constantly working behind the scenes on your behalf. Secondly, you should never make rash decisions while under pressure. This will usually cause you to make the wrong decisions based on how you are feeling at that moment. The process can have you feeling isolated, fearful, and overwhelmed by the ongoing pressure from others. While riding the storm, you can also experience a lack and betrayal by others. In those moments of isolation, be still so you can hear from God. Don't let the fear-inducing circumstances take you to your limits. Just believe in God even while you are under pressure. Through the storm, wait to hear from God, be dependent on Him, not others, and don't give in to what your flesh desires.

The older I get, the more I see the importance of seeking God in all my decisions. Walking in God's obedience makes the road easier and more fulfilling to travel. Sometimes the road is hard, but we only need to make the first step and let God do the rest. You see, your dream can be your reality when you involve God and allow Him to show you the pathway to get to it.

What are some dreams and desires you are holding in your heart?

____

____

____

Are there things you are hiding inside or beating yourself up about wishing you had gone in another direction?

____

____

____

Believe in God for the dreams He has placed in your heart and move forward to become the person He has called you to be and to fulfill the destiny He has placed on your life. When you dream, it gives you a different perspective and allows you to think beyond your current circumstances. Dream big, believe for bigger, and watch God move on your behalf in your life.

Can you trust God and start dreaming again? The future you see is the future you will get, but you must walk it out.

Your Reality

Reality: The world or state of things as they exist, as opposed to an idealistic or notional idea of them.

When life's reality sets in, it can be a real wake-up call as the realization of your present is in direct opposition to your dream. Becoming a wife and mother, and managing a home and a job can be overwhelming. Who do you turn to? Your parents, and friends, or do you keep it tucked away, afraid to tell anyone? The Lord wants to be the one you come to first. I have learned that when I give it all to Him, He works through the situation with all that I need. He will put those in your life to help you get through, but you must trust Him. ***Psalm 18:2 says, "The Lord is my rock, and my fortress, and my deliverer; my God, my strength, in whom I will trust; my buckler, and the horn of my salvation, and my high tower" (KJV).*** God is your strength, not man, friend, or foe. His word says He is our rock, and we must trust Him.

Even when you can't see the end, you must trust that He has your best interest at heart. The reality is you must walk through the situation knowing you will come out victorious in the end. Although this may not be easy, it will involve some long-suffering and endurance. You are not walking by yourself when the Lord is a part of your life. God is bigger than any situation you are facing; give Him all the focus instead of focusing on the problem. For example, to be a long-distance runner, one must build up the endurance to do so. It takes practice and conditioning of the body, trust, and direction. No one can run a marathon without training, just as learning to trust and endure will require you to take the first step and endure until God changes the situation.

The truth is when I gave up and succumbed to the exhaustion that was my life, God was right there, carrying me when I couldn't carry myself. Sometimes when I think about what I now call my former life, I just say, "Thank you, Lord, for bringing me through," "for letting me live to see tomorrow." So many women in abusive relationships don't live to see tomorrow, and I am grateful I survived and can share the story.

One in every four women will experience domestic violence in her lifetime, 85% of domestic violence victims are women, and 1.3 million women are victims of physical assault each year by an intimate partner, with most cases never being reported to the police, as reported by the National Coalition of Domestic Violence. The statistics are horrifying, but as I went through the abuse, I, too, was one who never reported it. I told myself it would make the situation worse because the military would have intervened, he would have gotten into trouble, and it would have negatively affected the family. The truth is I was just scared, scared of the unknown, scared of being alone with my children with no one to help me. I recall an evening we were all at a friend's house, and a situation escalated to the point I was punched in the eye. The impact was such that blood splattered everywhere, and as I tried to attend to my face while masking the embarrassment, he took the kids and left. Our friends drove me to the hospital because I needed a stitch or two, but I was too afraid to go in. I instead had them take me home, where I packed up my things and the kids and left town to be with family. After about a week, I came back home, and after the usual promises, things were good for a while. But of course, it didn't last.

My reality was I was in a bad relationship that was so far out of control I was helpless as to what I should do. We had moved once again, and now I was even farther away from family. Feeling stuck and alone, I continued to tolerate the abuse, and things never got better, only worse. What do you do when you are trying to cope with the situation you are in? You get in survival mode, doing whatever is necessary to merely survive. I realized that whenever he drank, the fights and arguments were much worse. My survival tactics led me to start drinking because it gave me the courage to stand up to him. I knew I could not win, but I felt it put me on a different playing field with him. I now realize it was the wrong thing to do, but it was how I coped with my reality. I needed the Lord more than ever, but He was the furthest thing from my mind. I am so glad that God doesn't throw us away as we do Him. Instead of trying to figure out how to fix the mess that was called my life, I should have been running to the Lord and laying all my problems at his feet. Instead, I took it all on myself, and the problems didn't get smaller; they grew larger. How do you react when going through an unpleasant situation? Do you turn to the Lord, or do you try to find answers from others? Do you trust the opinions of man more than the promises of the Lord? I did. One of the things that the Lord revealed to me is that I put my relationship with my now ex-husband before my relationship with Him. I was more consumed with the earthly relationship that I sacrificed the most important relationship that I should have, that is, my relationship with the Lord.

I needed to trust in the Lord as the word tells us to do. *Proverbs 3:5-6 says, "Trust in the Lord with all thy heart; and lean not unto thy own understanding. In all thy ways, acknowledge Him, and He shall direct thy paths" (KJV).* Trust can be a hard thing to do when you have been hurt by people who you call family or friends. There is a level of discomfort in the unknown, but God wants you to trust Him despite what you see or how you feel and to be in total submission. This is hard when the demands of life pull you in other directions, but the state of your current relationship with the Lord will dictate how open you are to doing this. When you can trust the Lord in all areas of your life, you will experience peace and joy. In moments of doubt, release it quickly, give it to the Lord, and let Him handle the situation. When your situation looks hopeless, you must look to the Lord to be your strength. Although this may not be your automatic response, it will be a training process for your mind. As situations arise, the process should get easier as you grow in your relationship with the Lord. When I stopped trying to do it myself, the Lord revealed things to me. When I let go, I started to see Him move, and my life began to change for the better. He further equipped me for the reality I was living in and provided me an exit ramp from my present journey, making me stronger and better than I could have ever imagined.

Reflect on those things that are not what you want them to be and ask yourself these questions:

Have you faced the reality of your current situation?

____

Do you feel deep in your heart that this is where God wants you to be?

____

____

How can you apply God's word to this situation?

____

____

____

Do you trust God as Proverbs 3:5-6 tells us to do?

____

____

____

What steps can you take in your life to put total trust in Him now?

____

____

Jeremiah 29:11 says, "For I know the plans I have for you, declares the Lord, plans to prosper you and not to harm you, plans to give you hope and a future." You must trust God for your future, as He knows what is best for you. One of the songs that really helped me through some of the hardest moments of my life was Yolanda Adam's "The Battle is the Lord's." I had to keep reminding myself that God is for me and that He is with me even when I can't feel it. Give your burdens to the Lord and seek Him for the answers to all your questions about the reality you are living in. Be aware of the many ways the Lord may speak to you. If not, directly it can be through others, visions, and dreams. Be aware of the people around you and those that He may move away from you. He is concerned about every detail of your life; you must trust Him on what those plans are for you.

How close or far is your present reality to your dreams of how you want it to be?

____

____

____

Do you feel you can trust God for His leading?

If you cannot, what is hindering your trust?

____

____

____

Is there anything that is stopping you from trusting God in this situation?

____

____

____

When your reality is nothing like your dream, assess yourself and the situation you are in. Are you walking with the Lord and seeking Him for guidance? Sometimes your dreams are not His dreams for your life. In my case, I was praying for something that didn't happen in my past relationship, but I am now experiencing it in my current one. The dream has happened, just not the way I thought it would. When you seek God, it can shift your thinking so that your desires line up with His desires for you. Just know that when you follow the Lord, your dreams can become your reality sometimes in a way that you never expected.

The Pain & Heartbreak

Pain & Heartbreak: Physical and mental suffering or discomfort; overwhelming distress.

Pain, whether it be physical or mental, is nothing we enjoy. Along with heartbreak, it can be a devastating process if not properly equipped to handle the situation. What equips us to be able to handle the pain? When we know the word of God and realize that He is all we need. *John 16:33 says, "These things I have spoken unto you, that in me ye might have peace. In the world ye shall have tribulation: but be of good cheer; I have overcome the world (KJV).*

Have you ever wondered why God allows pain to enter our lives? It is something that we can't run or hide from. One of the most painful times in my life was losing my mother. Up to that point, what I thought had been bad, the abuse and affairs paled to the pain I felt with her passing. As I dealt with the pain of heart-wrenching loss, there was still the ever-present pain of the broken relationship I was currently in. How could the one who said I love you put me through the things I had and was experiencing?

The pain of a broken relationship, still lingering

The pain of losing my mother, still fresh

The pain of trying to move forward and feeling stuck, my struggle

Physical pain affects the body, while mental pain tortures the mind. When I think back to the physical pain of the abuse, I can now thank God for keeping me alive and bringing me out of that relationship. My mind reflects on the years of hiding the black eyes and bruises experienced as I went through the process of surviving. I thought I alone could change things, change him, and make the marriage better, but it never happened. I thought God would be angry with me if I divorced to get out of the situation, and most of all, I didn't want to disappoint God. I wanted Him to honor my prayers and change my marriage. How long did it take for me to realize that my plans and God's plans were never in sync? Too long, I must say, and I have learned to pray the prayer that God's will be done and that He prepares me for whatever his will is. On the outside, I had gotten so good at hiding the pain and wearing the mask to convince everyone that I was happy, while on the inside, I was broken to the point that only God could rescue me.

When we are in pain, we need to seek God for healing. We need to realize that He is all we need and learn how to lean on Him. Pain will draw us closer to God as we realize that we cannot do this alone. *I Peter 5:7 says, casting all your care upon Him; for He careth for you (KJV).* Give God your worries, give Him your pain, and every situation in your life because you can't handle it on your own. Whether it is the pain from a loss, the pain of an affair, or the pain from abuse, give it all to God, for He is the only one that can heal you, and He cares for you.

When I lost my mother, I didn't deal with the pain. I shut myself off from the world, and I pulled away from God. I shut myself off from everyone and even pulled away from the church. I just existed by waking up in the morning, going to work, coming home, and doing what needed to be done around the house, and before I knew it, a year had passed, and everyone who had been around me was gone. I allowed myself to be angry, but by pulling away from God, I only hurt myself in the end. I let my pain consume me instead of letting God consume my pain. It seemed to be the last straw for me because of what I was already dealing with in my marriage. But you do what you must, our coping mechanism, so to speak, to just get through the situation you are in, which is survival mode. What were the reasons behind why I stayed in a relationship that was so unhealthy for my family and me? As I reflect on that time, I really wanted things to work out. I also worried about my children, not wanting to make things harder on them with regard to potentially struggling financially. Now on the other side of that pain, I must ask myself, did I really trust God in all of that? No. I had to realize I was not alone and that God was with me and that God is for me, but I didn't see that. *In Hebrews 13:5, God says, "Never will I leave you; never will I forsake you."* Even when I pulled away from God, He never left me. He waited for me to let Him work through the pain. I won't allow myself to go to that place again because I know who I am in God and who I am always.

Sometimes I wonder if I had missed a way out, overlooked something, or someone who had wanted to help, and by doing so, had gone through a season of pain and heartbreak longer than I was supposed to. Could things have been different? What I realize is that It was my cross to bear, and without it, I would not have a story to tell and would not have the skills to be able to help someone else get through this same situation and be a testimony of God's goodness towards us. I cannot be angry about my trials and tribulations; I now know they made me stronger and better than I was before. These trials brought me closer to God, to see Him in all of my mess, to learn to depend on Him, and always look to Him to heal the pain and get rid of the heartbreak. How many people give up before they ever start living the life that God has planned for them? How many get caught up in the pain and the heartbreak and never recover from it? My prayer for you today is that you deal with the pain and heartbreak by calling on the Lord and letting him show you the way to start the journey to your healing process.

What are some things in your life currently that are causing you pain?

____

____

____

How are you coping with them?

____

____

____

Do you believe that God is for you and is with you always as Hebrews 13:5 tells us? Why or why not?

____

____

____

Do you see how God can use your pain to help others?

____

____

____

____

____

____

My favorite chapter to read in the Bible is Psalm 91. It is my reminder of who is in control of my life and is the only one in which I can find shelter. This would be a good chapter for you to read daily and memorize it if possible to keep it in your spirit. Verse 2 of Psalms 91 says, "He is my refuge and my fortress, my God, in whom I trust." It ends with verses 14-16 that say, "Because He loves me," says the Lord, "I will rescue him; I will protect him, for he acknowledges my name. He will call upon me, and I will answer him, I will be with him in trouble, I will deliver him and honor him. With long life will I satisfy him and show him my salvation."

Don't let your situation make you helpless; overcome the situation. Move forward even when things seem too hard and walk into your destiny just as God has planned it. One step at a time, and as time passes, you will be ready to take more. The change may not come overnight, but it will come; you just must be patient. God loves you very much and is concerned about everything that concerns you, whether big or small. Even when we forget about Him, He never forgets about us. I am so glad that God doesn't put us on the back burner as we do Him sometimes. Trust Him, believe what the word says, let go of the pain, and lay all your worries at His feet. Whether you see things changing or not, stand firm in the faith, believing that God is working it all out on your behalf.

The Brokenness Inside

Brokenness: The characteristic of being broken.

To pick up the pieces, one must first understand that something is broken. Being broken spiritually puts us in a place where we can hear from God and are open to His intervention, as He is the only source we should turn to. In this time of brokenness, we experience God the way we should all the time, not just in this time of need. We are totally dependent on Him, and through the storm, our relationship grows stronger, and we put ourselves in a place where we can then learn the lessons from the storm, even if we don't recognize it at first. *Psalm 147:3 says, "He healeth the broken in heart, and bindeth up their wounds" (KJV).*

When I look back over my life, I realize that I had to get to the point of recognizing and admitting my brokenness before I could begin the process of allowing God to heal me. We are human, and because of this, it is our first instinct to fix the situation ourselves. Time after time, we put our hands in our mess to try to fix it instead of turning to the One who can fix it all. Oftentimes we make things worse with our meddling, and then God allows us to fall on our face from our controlling tactics. Once we fall, He can then come and reassemble our broken pieces. Sometimes the reassembly takes longer than originally planned because of our failure to surrender.

I thought I could fix my marriage on my own by compromising who I was, and what I wanted and desired instead of remaining silent just to keep the peace. In doing so, I was disrespected, and mistreated and I lost "me" in the process. I eventually hit rock bottom and stopped caring about myself. I went to work, took care of my children, and maintained my household while in a fog of depression. I compromised who I was and what I believed. I had given up on ever being happy and began to settle and accept where I was. The one thing with settling is when God has a purpose and a destiny for your life; you won't be allowed to settle. I don't really remember how long this went on, but when I became aware and realized I couldn't do it on my own, it was then that God began to minister to me. It was then that I realized God was all that I needed- my refuge and my strength.

Amid my brokenness, I heard the voice of God, and I began to experience His love toward me.

In the midst of my brokenness, God changed me and made me into the woman I needed to be and showed me the steps to take toward living out my purpose by putting Him first and foremost in my life.

During my brokenness, God showed me that I am worth much more than I thought I was worth and that His love is all that I need.

And in this state of brokenness, God brought life into a lifeless body and healed my broken heart. From this experience, I learned to always seek Him first in all that I do, so as to never be put in a place of brokenness again.

Read Colossians 2:6-15 (NIV) below:

So then, just as you received God Jesus as Lord, continue to live in Him, rooted and built up in Him, strengthened in the faith as you were taught, and overflowing with thankfulness. See to it that no one takes you captive through hollow and deceptive philosophy, which depends on human tradition and the basic principles of this world rather than on God. For in God, all the fullness of the Deity lives in bodily form, and you have been given fullness in God, who is the head over every power and authority. In Him you were also circumcised, in the putting off of the sinful nature, not with a circumcision done by the hands of men but with the circumcision done by God, having been buried with him in baptism and raised with him through your faith in the power of God, who raised him from the dead.

When you were dead in your sins and in the uncircumcision of your sinful nature, God made you alive with God. He forgave us all our sins, having canceled the written code, with its regulations, that was against us and that stood opposed to us; he took it away, nailing it to the cross. And having disarmed the powers and authorities, he made a public spectacle of them, triumphing over them by the cross.

What you can glean from these verses is that if you are in God, you should continue to put Him first to stay strengthened in your faith. Don't allow others to deceive you in the things of this world but continue to believe in the things of God. Life is hard and can be overwhelming at times, but the same God that raised Jesus from the grave is the same God who will take the stresses of this world and carry them on His shoulders, so you don't have to.

What I learned from these verses is that since I have received God, I need to walk in Him. You don't just wake up one day and have it all together; there is some soul searching, crying, and on-your-knee conversations with the Lord. This is something that needs to be worked on daily. My relationship with God is important, and I should not let anyone deter me away from His principles and His ways. I am complete with God, not broken, and all my sins were washed away the day I confessed my sins and asked God into my heart. I was dead in sin but am alive in God because of obedience and baptism of the Holy Ghost.

If you walk with God and stay rooted in Him, all blessings will flow through Him. With God, you are made whole; you are cleansed and have been given new life. You are alive, and as Isaiah 54 says, no weapons formed against you will prosper. God is your healer, and with Him, all things are possible, and you can have all that you need. Jehovah Rapha, our healer, and our refuge.

What things are you carrying around that are putting you in a state of brokenness?

____

____

____

How hard is it to give them over to God?

____

What steps will you take to try?

____

____

____

Did you learn anything about yourself in Colossians 2: 6-15?

____

____

____

____

____

____

Know that God's process for us always leads us to a greater good. We are in the fight to win and to overcome; remember, no storm lasts forever. And if we overcome, there is a blessing to inherit when the storm is all over.

Forgiveness of Wrongdoing

Forgiveness: A conscious, deliberate decision to release feelings of resentment or vengeance toward a person who has harmed you, regardless of whether they deserve it or not.

To move forward into your new beginnings and the process of healing, you must forgive those who have wronged you and brought pain into your life. Not being able to forgive can cause you to have a hardness of heart and block the blessings that the Lord may have in store for you. *Ephesians 4:32 tells us to "Be ye kind to one another, tenderhearted, forgiving one another, even as Christ for God's sake has forgiven you (KJV).* You must forgive others just as God has forgiven you. We have all done things that warrant forgiving. Forgiveness is an act of mercy, and mercy is compassion that is shown to others. It allows you to be able to move forward; otherwise, you will be stuck in the past, miserable and unable to go forward, only backward, while the one you are unable to forgive goes on living their life.

Forgiveness was something I really struggled with for a long time. I wanted to forgive because I knew that it was what God wanted and commanded me to do, but the hurt was so deep I found myself not wanting to forgive but instead wanting the one who had hurt me for so long to feel the same pain, the deep pain that was inflicted on me, in his life. It took years of prayer on my part, and so many times when I thought I really had forgiven the wrong that was done to me, I found that I hadn't. I was stuck and unable to move forward because of resentment of what I had and was experiencing in my life.

This one act, that act of forgiveness, was keeping me from my healing process. I can honestly say I hated my husband and the marriage I was in, and for years I harbored the hatred. How do you forgive someone who caused you so much emotional and physical pain, who took something as sacred as marriage and lived it as if it were a game? How do you forgive the act of adultery, which brought a child into your life, that was not your own? And how do you love that child, because it wasn't the child's fault that they are here but is a reminder of the infidelity that took place? You can only do it with the grace that God extends to you each day. God's grace allows you to forgive and is the empowerment of God. When we forgive, we display God's grace. Forgiveness deals with the heart, and we should forgive completely. Forgiveness is a process, and it is up to you as to how long your process will take. Are you willing to let go and let God take control of your heart and mind because the two go hand in hand? My process took years because I was unable to get over the pain that I was experiencing year after year.

How was I able to move forward and love a child that was not my own? It was God's grace that He extended to me. The Lord brought to my memory how a specific woman loved me, and I was not her own. You see, I was a child born outside of the bond of marriage to a man who already had a wife. I don't know all the details of the relationship, and I didn't grow up with my biological father or siblings I found out I had years later when I was at an age to inquire about it. The excitement of meeting them for the first time was also filled with fear as I then knew the circumstances surrounding my birth. I was most afraid to meet the mother of my siblings; how would she react or feel about me? I was that child who was not her own, and this is what the Lord brought to my memory as I sat thinking about the child and the situation that I was now faced with.

The rest of the story went like this; we met, and she embraced me with such love and acceptance that I had my answer of how to handle the situation I was in. I loved and cared for the child as if my own. I chose to show the love of God, that which was shown to me so many years before. It didn't matter what anyone else thought; I knew I was doing the right thing, that which God has called all of us to do, to love as He has loved us unconditionally.

If it had not been for the Lord, I would not have been able to do what I did. If I hadn't been concerned with pleasing the Lord, I could not have done it, and if I had not learned how to forgive, it would have been impossible for me to move forward. The moment I was able to forgive, the weight of all I had been carrying fell off me. It was a freeing experience that allowed God to then start the healing process within me, for Him to show me that everything was going to be alright. My life may not have been the way I wanted it to be or thought it should be, but it was the way God wanted it to be. God worked it all out for my good, and just as the word says, the work that He has begun in me will continue until the end until I have completed the task given to me.

Forgive so that you can be healed – What wounds are festering inside of you that are stopping your healing process?

____

____

Forgive so that you can move forward – What is that memory or event that is holding you back from moving forward?

____

____

Forgive so that you can see life anew – What do you want for the future?

____

____

Do you believe in God for those things?

____

____

Are there things that you feel guilty about - or feel you need to be forgiven? Is that hindering your forgiveness of others?

____

____

Forgive so that the grace of God will take you places you never dreamed of – Does your prayer life line up with God's word and the plans you think He has for you? How much time do you spend in prayer daily?

____

____

Forgive because it's what God expects you to do – List the names/events of people/things you need to forgive and pray God works on your heart.

Come back to this page and check off your
progress.

1. _______________________________

2. _______________________________

3. _______________________________

I was listening to the radio, and the
discussion was on unforgiveness. There
had been a study done that classified it as
being a disease in the medical text. The
article titled "The Deadly Consequences of
Unforgiveness" by Lorie Johnson (CBN
News Medical Reporter), said according to
Dr. Steven Standiford, the chief of
surgery at the Cancer Treatment Centers
of America, refusing to forgive can make
people sick and keep them ill. Because of
this, forgiveness therapy is now being used
to help treat diseases.

Pastor and author of the book "The Forgiveness Project," Dr. Michael Barry, stated that of all cancer patients, 61 percent have forgiveness issues, and of those, more than half are severe. By harboring anger and hatred, it creates a state of chronic anxiety, which produces excess adrenaline and cortisol, which depletes the production of natural killer cells, which is what the body uses to fight against cancer. Dr. Barry says the first step in learning to forgive is to realize how much God has forgiven us. What a powerful statement! I believe we sometimes forget about the wrong that we have done daily and how much forgiveness God extends to us.

When you forgive, you find peace, and when you are at peace, the love of God can flow in you and through you. Read Matthew chapter 18. This gives us the standard on how we should forgive. How many times did Jesus say you should forgive your brother? _________________. And if you don't forgive from the heart, how will our heavenly father treat you?

____

____

The Healing Process

Healing: To make whole; the process of restoration, mending back together; whether physical or mental.

Only after you have learned how to forgive can your healing begin. When you are unable to forgive, it keeps you in a place of anger and hurt, playing the offense over in your head, things that will slow the healing process down. When going through the healing process, whether it is physical, mental, low self-esteem, or a broken relationship, you have to believe that you will be healed. *Psalm 34:18 tells us, The LORD is nigh unto them that are of a broken heart, and saves such as be of a contrite spirit" (KJV).*   You need the Lord to restore you and make you whole again. This is not something you can do on your own. You must turn it over to the Lord by simply laying it at His feet and not worrying about it anymore and just allowing Him to guide you through the process. Let's look at the word restore. To **restore** means to renew, revive, reestablish, and return to its formal, original, or normal condition.

When God restores, it is better than it was before.

As I started this process, I had no idea it would be such a long journey for me. My self-esteem had hit rock bottom, and the first step in my healing process was to start loving myself the way the Lord loved me. Just getting up and taking the time to do my hair and makeup, and caring about the way that I looked, was a process for me. I had allowed someone to make me feel like I had no worth, that I wasn't enough, and that I wasn't loved. I had forgotten about the only one that mattered, God loved me, and that should have been enough, but instead, I was looking to man, my husband, for the love that I thought I needed.

What are some examples of things we need to be healed from? Personally, those things from which I had to be healed were:

1.   Mental & Physical Abuse (Takes away self-esteem, self-worth, and fosters anger)

2.   Physical manifestations of depression (Takes

away your self-sufficiency, possibly developing a codependent relationship with medication and people)

3. Broken relationships (non-sustaining marriages or friendships)

4. Loss of a loved one or friend

What Psalm 34:18 tells me is that at my lowest, I am never alone; the Lord is with me. I may feel isolated, frustrated, and without hope, consumed with the feeling that I am all alone, but that's not the case. The Lord is with us all when our hearts are broken and our darkest days are upon us.

When we are broken spiritually, it puts us in a place where we can hear from God and are open to Him intervening because we realize He is the only one we can turn to. I believe that when we are broken, we do hear from God because we are sensitive to His voice and are open to His way of doing things.

In this time of brokenness, we experience God the way we should all the time being open to His leading in our situation, taking our hands off in total dependence on Him.

Starting the healing process involves three things:

1. Cultivate our relationship with the Lord

   You cultivate your relationship with the Lord through prayer and reading of the scripture. *John 15:5 says, "I am the vine; you are the branches. If a man remains in me and I in him, he will bear much fruit; apart from me, you can do nothing."* This is where your relationship starts. This may be difficult in the beginning if you have not been disciplined in doing so, be patient with yourself. One thing to remember is we are nothing without God. If we remain in God, we can do anything, be anything. It is up to us to study the word and let God teach us through it. God will allow different situations in our lives to show us yet another side of Himself and eventually show us that self-reliance will always be unsuccessful without Him. Although some situations may be uncomfortable, rest assured the situation will bring growth in you as well as draw you closer to God. There are some situations that make you run right to Him instead of running away. You should take time daily to pray and study, and not only will you become closer to God; but you will also strengthen yourself from the attacks of the enemy, even when the enemy may be those closest to us. As you develop your relationship with the Lord, it will help you in your relationships with others. If you do not have a relationship with the Lord, then your journey starts there. To cultivate this relationship, you must first accept Him as your Lord and Savior, which will change your heart and mind forever. If you would like to accept God you're your heart, follow the steps below.

Romans 4:23 says, ***"For all have sinned and fall short of the glory of God."*** (Confess with your mouth that you are a sinner).

Romans 5:8, "But God commanded his love toward us, in that, while we were yet sinners, Christ died for us. (Believe in your heart that Christ died for you).

Romans 6:23, "For the wages of sin is death; but the gift of God is eternal life through Jesus Christ our Lord." (Ask Jesus Christ to come into your heart).

Romans 10:13, "For whoever calls upon the name of the Lord shall be saved." (You will have everlasting life with Him).

2. Forgive those who have hurt us

Forgiveness is an act of mercy, and mercy is compassion that is shown to others. You must forgive, just as Christ has forgiven you. *Ephesians 4:32 tells us to "Be ye kind to one another, tenderhearted, forgiving one another, even as Christ for God's sake has forgiven you.* Although hard, this will be the most rewarding and peace-producing lesson you will ever learn. It is neither acceptance nor agreement with the person or the action but a way to show true obedience to God's word. Forgiveness allows you to be free from the anger that will keep you from moving forward and receiving peace, as well as the blessings that God has for you. Forgiveness was something that I really struggled with when dealing with the pain from the physical abuse I suffered at the hands of someone else. I knew that God wanted and commanded me to forgive, but the hurt was so deep that all I wanted was for that person to feel the way that I felt, the pain that cut so deep inside of me. This one act, the act of forgiveness, was keeping me from my healing process, and it took years for me to forgive and move forward with my life. I remember the morning I woke up and felt so free. I knew at that moment; that I had forgiven him. One Sunday during church service, the Lord revealed to me that the time was now to express that I had forgiven him. As hard as it was, I did it, and the peace that I had afterward made me wish I had been able to do it sooner.

3. Share our story with others

Sharing your story with someone else cannot only benefit you from sharing but also can help someone else through their process. Your story is not to be kept to yourself because you never know who it will help, including you in the process. As embarrassing as it may seem, you will learn that your situation was not as unique as you may have thought. Part of my healing process involved sharing my story with others. I was embarrassed at first and had become a master at masking what was really going on in my life. I remember being approached by a friend who had just found out that her husband had cheated, and because of the infidelity, a baby was on the way. She didn't know that I had experienced this same thing because I had not spoken of it, and she just needed to talk it out with someone. At that moment, I said to myself, "Lord, I know you are not going to make me share." I then proceeded to tell her my story, and of course, she was shocked. I shared with her my feelings, the good, the bad, and the ugly, but expressed that she needed to seek God through all of it before she decided what her next steps would be. Sharing my story with her let her know she wasn't

alone in this walk and this trial that she
was going through.

What are the things you need healing from? Only
you can fill in the blank and then decide to start
your healing process today. Don't put it off any
longer.......................................

List 5 things you can do in your daily life to
build up your self-esteem.

1. _______________________________________

____

2. _______________________________________

____

3. _______________________________________

____

4. _______________________________________

____

5. _______________________________________

____

Prayer to make it through

Prayer: A solemn petition to God; a form of worship, public or private.

To have any type of relationship with God, you need to make prayer a priority. Prayer is a conversation, just you and God as if He was sitting beside you in the room. As you grow in your walk with God, so will your prayers. Prayer will get you through your current situation, even when you feel that you can't take another step, take another breath, or shield another blow. Set aside time daily for prayer, and it doesn't hurt to have a special place designated for prayer also. *Matthew 6:6 says, "But when you pray, go into your room, close the door, and pray to your Father, who is unseen. Then you're Father, who sees what is done in secret, will reward you" (KJV).*

Your prayer life, whether written or verbal, is important to God. Pray without ceasing and seek God for everything. With your prayer life in place, you have one of the weapons that you need to fight the enemy. You have to remember that everything you go through is for a purpose, to shape and mold you into the person that God wants you to be and to prepare you for what He has in store for you. Your mindset will change to align with God's desire for you. No one can take it away, and you should seek God for all wisdom and understanding. He only wants to be close to you, and through prayer and the reading of the word, you can have the most special relationship of your life.

As I was going through my situation, sometimes things were so hard I couldn't pray. There were times when I was so angry because of the situation that I didn't want to pray. I spent so much time being angry at God; wasted time that I am sure I delayed the relationship and peace that I now have in Him. Even now, I find at times when I cannot pray; I worship in song. There have been times when I have worshiped for hours, alone in my car or at home, because I didn't know what to say or hurt so bad that words escaped me. Still, in those times of worship, I felt the strong presence of God in my life.

Prayer brought me closer to God, and His word gave me the strength that I need to move forward into my purpose, those things that are for me and me only. By developing a relationship with God, I can ensure the decisions that I make are ordered by Him. I understand that God is everything and is in control of my life now. I receive peace in the confidence that all my needs and my family's needs are taken care of. I am grateful, and I know I could never repay God for all that He has done for me.

Don't let the enemy get you to a place where you will become mute to God. That is exactly where the enemy wants you to be because if you are angry and unable to communicate with God, then you open the door for the enemy to feed you lies. Constant communication with God helps you remember who you are as a person and who you are in Him. Have you ever heard the saying, "When life gives you lemons, turn them into lemonade"? Just know that God will take the lemons in your life and turn them into glasses of ice-cold lemonade. The Bible tells us that *ALL* things work together for our good;

it doesn't say some of them, but *ALL* of them. No matter how bad the situation is or was, God will turn it around for your good. Pray without ceasing, turn your thinking to claim victory over your situation, and continually confess the promises of God until you see them manifest in your life. Be patient and watch God move in your life as only He can.

Prayer changes things

Prayer keeps your communication open with God

Prayer strengthens you, protects you in times of trouble

Prayer encourages you and gives you peace

Prayer opens doors that God wants to open and closes the ones that need to be closed

I thank God for giving me this avenue of communication with Him

Dedicate a set time for the next ten days to prayer in an effort to grow your relationship with God and get the strength you need to sustain yourself and keep yourself at peace.

Day	Date	Time

God's Love

Love: To regard with affection; to like, to delight in.

The greatest example of love was God giving his son as a living sacrifice. *John 3:16 says, "For God so loved the world, that He gave his only begotten Son, that whosoever believeth in him should not perish, but have everlasting life" (KJV).* The greatest sacrifice of love was made for you and me so that we might live and not die. Too many times, we try to find love in tangible things and people without looking to the one who understands and loves us unconditionally. *In Matthew 22:37, Jesus tells us, "Thou shall love the Lord thy God with all your heart, and with all your soul, and with all your mind (KJV).* We should love God the way He loves us, with agape love. Agape love is kindhearted, peacemaking, and unquestioning. If we can show agape love to others, our lives will be impacted forever.

Because God loved me so much, He opened up a door for my children to start attending a church that had a bus ministry to come and pick them up on Sunday. That was the beginning of my turnaround, though I didn't yet know it. Through that bus ministry and the people God used to operate it, I saw the fire and enjoyment that my children had, just being a part of it. Eventually, I gave my life to the Lord and started attending church with my children. That is where my true growth began, as I learned how to trust God and place everything in his hands. It wasn't as easy as it sounds, but I went through my process. Although my process took years, I know God's hand was on me every step of the way. For me, the process took a while because I had to learn how to love the Lord and the relationship that I could have with Him. I also had to learn how to love myself just as God loved me. I had lost all confidence in myself and had to start over, like a newborn learning to crawl before they could walk. I was hard on myself for staying in that marriage, and I was also embarrassed that I had allowed these things to happen. Looking back today, I am grateful that God loved me so much that He didn't allow the situation to kill me. Many victims of abuse are no longer alive.

Sometimes things can change in an instant, and at other times it can take weeks, months, or years. Whatever your process, don't give up or get discouraged. That is what the enemy wants you to do. We get discouraged when things don't happen as quickly or in the manner we want them. My discouragement came when I didn't see things change, at least in the marriage and in the man himself. We never look at ourselves when something is wrong to see what it is that we may need to change ourselves. I do realize that change was taking place, but it was within me. I am not the same woman I was back then. I have learned that my relationship with God takes precedence over everything else. My walk includes putting God first and family second throughout my process. Never put anyone on a pedestal to try to please them more than God.

The life that God wants you to live is so much more than you could ever imagine or dream. Where we fall short is not having the faith and patience to sustain the wait. If we don't see it or know how the story ends, we tend to get discouraged quickly and try to take matters into our own hands. Just as, for example, getting into shape takes time, so have patience, and allow God to move in His timing. Believing God for the things we want and those things that He wants for us is a process. We mess up when we don't walk the process out according to God's plan but instead try to take shortcuts. The process shapes us into the people God wants us to be and prepares us for the blessings that He has in store for our lives.

Galatians 3:6 says, "In the same way, Abraham believed God, and God counted him as righteous because of his faith." Faith is the doorway to activating and receiving the blessings of God. God not only loves us but also wants to bless us and bless those that we love in the process. The word bless is used 516 times in the Bible, and because of the covenant God had with Abraham, God bestowed certain blessings on him and his descendants. If you belong to God, then you too are a recipient of the "Blessings of Abraham" and have the right to receive those blessings that God has promised us. Blessings are tangible and transferable. They are a present reality in the spiritual realms that are to be given and received. Galatians 3:9 goes on to say that all who put their faith in God share the same blessing Abraham received because of his faith. God already has our success, prosperity, and fulfillment all planned out; we just need to follow His directions in his word, have faith, and love Him as much as He loves us.

John 15: 16 says, "You did not choose me, but I chose you and appointed you to go and bear fruit – fruit that will last. Then the Father will give you whatever you ask in my name."

This verse explains to us that God chose us, not because of anything that we have done but simply because He loves us. We just need to be obedient to what He is asking us to do, and we can receive whatever we ask for in His name.

What does this verse say that we should do?

____

____

____

Does this verse make you feel that you are loved by God? Why or why not?

____

   Dr. Cynthia J. Moss

God's love will bless us (Think of a time God blessed you)

____

____

God's love will sustain us (Think of a time God made things happen that defied logic)

____

____

God's love will guide us (Think of a time God kept you from going in the wrong direction)

____

____

God's love will be our light in times of darkness (Think of a time when God brought you out of your sorrow)

____

____

God's love will pick us up when we are broken
(Think of a time when God picked you up)

____

____

God's love will hold us when we are lonely (Think
of a time when you know God was there when
nobody else was)

____

____

If not for his love, where would I be? Where would
you be?

____

____

____

____

____

God's Grace

Grace: The free and unmerited favor of God.

God's grace is nothing that we can earn. He gives it to us freely, and it is by His grace that we can say "We made it through" and not by our own actions. Grace is God's divine ability that he imparts to us to do what we cannot do on our own. ***Psalm 84:11 says, "For the Lord God is a sun and shield: the Lord will give peace and glory: no good thing will he withhold from them that walk uprightly (KJV).*** There is nothing that He won't do for us; all that is required is to walk honorably before Him. If it wasn't for His grace, I don't know where I would be. God's grace kept me safe when I needed protection, sane when I thought I would lose my mind, strong when I felt I didn't have the strength to fight, and divine enablement to hang in there even when my situation did not change.

There are times when I just wanted God to take away the pain and change the situation with a snap of a finger. What I learned is sometimes He will change the situation, and then there are other times where he will change you to give you strength to get through the process. *2nd Corinthians 12:9 says, "My grace is sufficient for you, for my power is made perfect in weakness." Therefore, I will boast all the more gladly about my weaknesses, so that God's power may rest on me".* When you can't change your circumstances, all you can do is rely on the sustaining grace of God. Ask God for help and hold on to His promises while filling your mind with His word. Though my process seemed long and hard, the growth that I see in myself and the change I've made into the woman that God wanted me to be and where He wanted to take me has allowed me to hold my head up and not be ashamed anymore. There were times I was so ashamed and embarrassed because others knew what was going on, the affair in particular, and people who were supposed to be my friends didn't say a word about it. Why didn't they tell me? I felt like crawling in a hole because of what I was experiencing and had been through, but now I can hold my head high and tell others that they can make it through.

God understands where you are, and He really

understands the situation, your situation. What He wants you to do is not be afraid and trust Him. He understands every emotion and wants you to work through them, His way, not yours. Remember, the things of God will never take you where the grace of God cannot sustain you. Grace, the unmerited favor of God, is sufficient and all that you need to get through any situation or circumstance that you may be experiencing at this very moment. Listen for God's voice to guide you and believe in faith that you will be victorious over the situation.

God's grace is new every day and never runs out. His grace will cover you; all you have to do is ask and then be open to receiving.

What is your definition of grace?

____

____

____

How accepting are you to receiving God's grace?

____

____

Do you feel that His grace can sustain you in any situation? Why or Why not?

____

____

In your personal life, how much grace do you extend to others who have hurt you?

____

____

In my daily prayer life, I ask and thank God for the grace and mercy that He extends to me daily. In your prayer life, try asking and thanking God for His grace and start to see how different your days become. As you start this journey of receiving and extending grace to others, things will change for you and your process. It is time to start seeing God as the loving one that He is and to start receiving all that He has for you.

Psalm 116:5

"The Lord is gracious and righteous; our God is full of compassion."

New Beginnings

As I step away from the mirror and start towards the steps to my new life, I can't help thinking about what happiness awaits my family and me. Starting over can be scary, so it is important that you move forward without hesitation and continue to trust God with the unknown.

When I was suffering physical abuse, adulterous affairs, and the life consequences of those situations, I never imagined that I would be so happy now and that it wasn't too late to start over. For so many years, I believed God could do all things, but I was so discouraged that I thought He just didn't want to do it for me. Boy, was I so wrong about that! You see, what I went through before is like a bad dream. It's all behind me now, and what I see in front of me is the new beginnings that God has planned out for me. Remember it is not over until God says it is, don't give up and keep the faith. If I had not experienced the loss, the absence of love, and the despair, I would not be able to appreciate what I have as fully as I do now.

Not only did He love me, but He also gave me the desires of my heart. What are some of these desires that God has given me? First, I have a new life with a new husband who loves God and loves me as he loves God, and our two families have become one. My prayer was always to fix the marriage that I was in, but my plan was not God's plan. And I am so happy that it worked out that my best wasn't what I thought it should be. You see if we can figure out what or how God is going to do something, then that isn't the way it is going to be done. I valued marriage and the relationship I was in, but it wasn't meant for me to be in that specific situation forever. It wasn't God's plan to change it, but instead, He changed me through the process. God has shown me the happiness you can feel when you are in a good healthy, loving relationship and that you can have the desires of your heart while living the life and the relationship you need to have with the Lord.

Second, I have completed my Doctoral degree, the 1st in my immediate family to do so. God has also given me a greater voice in ministry and, along with my husband, the ability to start a ministry together. I have my self-esteem back, and I am continually challenging my comfort zone more and more. I remain patient and prayerful for more blessings from God. I also feel God has given me more books to write, becoming a voice for all women who feel they are stuck and afraid.

Instead of being absorbed in the way we want our life to be, we should try asking God to show us His plan for our life. Ultimately His way is best, and you don't want to take a long way around to get to it. Start today trusting, believing, and aligning your thoughts with God's way of doing things. Submitting to the will of God allows something miraculous to happen. Life is limitless when God is in control and the head of your life.

As I start my new life with my new husband, I know that all things are possible because I have learned to put God first above all things. It doesn't mean I won't have challenges and additional growth opportunities, but it does mean that I will be victorious in them all. When people look at me now and know what I went through, they see the hand of God in my life. I am blessed to be in a place of happiness and to be an example of God's goodness. I have complete victory in my life because of the love of God.

Through it all, you have to begin to see yourself as God sees you. He created you, and you are beautiful. Love yourself as He loves you and never let anyone or anything define who you are, and in the end, you could be living your Cinderella story just as I have been given a chance to live mine.

God Made You Beautifully

When you look in the mirror, what do you see

Do you see the woman that God created you to be?

God made you beautiful and beautiful you are

To Him, you are His shining star

You were created in the likeness of God

To be holy and pure, to portray the image of God

Be not conformed to the things of this world

But instead, always stand on GOD'S HOLY WORD

Before you were, He knew you then

His heart you took, the earth stood still

His love for you will never change

Hold on tight, grab hold of the reins

God made you beautiful and beautiful you are

Never forget you are a PRINCESS TO GOD

"Being confident of this,
that he who began a good
work in you will carry it
on to completion until
the day of Christ Jesus"
Philippians 1:6

Acknowledgments

Special Thanks to:

My Lord and Savior for making me the woman I am today. Thank you for choosing me to be a part of your kingdom and for using me to be that vessel to help others and to show them the love that you have shown me, unconditional love.

My husband, Kenneth, thank you for seeing more in me than I saw in myself. For always pushing me to take that next step and opening my eyes to see bigger and better, to reach for the unreachable, and change the impossible. For knowing that with God by our side, nothing is impossible. We can accomplish every dream that God has laid in our hearts and fulfill every mission that God has given us to do.

My children Jessica, Robert, and Tiana, I thank God for you. The trials and tribulations we endured only made us stronger. Remember to keep God first, and you will always get through any situation that life will throw at you. My life was made better because you were a part of it.

Being a mother is the greatest honor the Lord could have ever bestowed upon me. Love you forever and always.

My stepchildren Christopher and Natalia, my daughters-in-law (Donna, and Jessica Ann), and my son-in-law (Vee, Jovanee), I thank God for enlarging my family. You will always hold a special place in my heart, and I look forward to the memories we will make together.

And to my grandchildren, words cannot express the love that I have for you. If being a mother wasn't enough happiness to experience, God gave me you, my superheroes, and my little princesses. I promise to be the best Mimmie ever and to guide you in the ways of the Lord always. Raiko, Elle, Madison, Leilani, Mia, Malachi, Maleia, Mason, Sarai, and Kehlani, May God protect you always.

And to my family and friends that supported me on this journey, and were there when I needed you, I thank you from the bottom of my heart.